AI and the Future of Healthcare

Revolutionizing Diagnosis and Treatment

Table of Contents

1. Introduction 1

2. AI: Redefining Healthcare 2

    2.1. An Introduction to AI in Healthcare 2

    2.2. AI for Diagnostics 2

    2.3. AI in Treatment Protocols and Personalized Medicine 3

    2.4. AI and Proactive Prevention 3

    2.5. Ethical Implications of AI 4

    2.6. The Future of AI in Healthcare 4

3. Diving into AI: A Fundamental Overview 6

    3.1. The Anatomy of AI 6

    3.2. AI Integrations into Healthcare 6

    3.3. AI in Disease Diagnosis 7

    3.4. AI in Treatment Protocols 7

    3.5. AI in Proactive Prevention 7

4. Machine Learning and Big Data in Medicine 9

    4.1. Understanding Machine Learning 9

    4.2. Big Data: Unleashing the Power of Information Overflow . . . 10

    4.3. Merging Machine Learning and Big Data in Healthcare 10

    4.4. Precision Medicine and Predictive Analytics 11

    4.5. Radiology and Imaging 11

    4.6. Drug Discovery and Development 12

    4.7. Future Prospects and Challenges 12

5. AI in Diagnostic Medicine: More Than a Second Opinion 14

    5.1. AI, Machine Learning, and Diagnostics 14

    5.2. Image Analysis and Its Potential 15

    5.3. Predictive Modelling in Disease Outbreaks 15

    5.4. Diagnosing Rare Diseases Using AI 16

    5.5. The Broadening Horizon of AI in Diagnostics 16

6. The AI Surgeon: Revolutionizing Surgical Precision 17

  6.1. AI in the Operation Theatre: An Introduction 17

  6.2. Robots Guided by AI: Unparalleled Precision 18

  6.3. Preoperative Planning: Paving Path for Success 18

  6.4. Perioperative Decision Making: Decoding Intraoperative Complexities 19

  6.5. Postoperative Evaluation and Follow-up: Optimizing Recovery 19

7. AI in Pharmacology: Personalizing Medication 21

  7.1. The Concept: Personalized Medication 21

  7.2. AI in Personalized Medication: The Bridge 21

  7.3. Case Study: AI in Oncology Pharmacogenomics 22

  7.4. The Promise and Perils of AI in Personalized Medication ... 23

  7.5. Future Outlook 23

8. Ethical Considerations of AI in Healthcare 25

  8.1. Ethical Concerns - An Overview 25

  8.2. Bias in Medical AI Systems 26

  8.3. Autonomy Vs. Oversight: Balancing the Scales 26

  8.4. Accountability and Transparency in AI 27

  8.5. Consent and Privacy 27

  8.6. The Promise of Ethical AI 28

9. AI and The Future of Mental Health 29

  9.1. Unmasking Mental Health with AI 29

  9.2. AI-Powered Therapy and Support 30

  9.3. Shrinking the Mental Health Treatment Gap 31

  9.4. The Ethics of AI in Mental Health 31

  9.5. AI: Shaping the Future of Mental Health 32

10. Breaking Barriers: AI in Global Healthcare 33

  10.1. Impact of AI on Global Healthcare 33

  10.2. AI Technologies Transforming Healthcare 33

10.3. Overcoming Challenges with AI in Healthcare 34

10.4. Future Prospects: AI's Growing Influence 35

11. Envisioning the Future: Prospects and Challenges of AI in Health 36

11.1. The Advent of AI in Healthcare: An Overview 36

11.2. The Future Outlook of AI in Healthcare 37

11.3. The Challenges and Limitations of AI 37

11.4. Mitigating Challenges for AI Success in Healthcare 38

Chapter 1. Introduction

Within this Special Report, we delve into a remarkable frontier where artificial intelligence (AI) merges with healthcare to transform the way we diagnose and treat health conditions. Even as we submerge into the depths of this technical discussion, we strive to keep it engaging, comprehensible, and firmly grounded in practical realities. Explore how AI, often referenced as a 'buzzword,' is pioneering revolution within the healthcare industry, intricately woven into systems for disease diagnosis, treatment protocols, and even proactive prevention. Despite its ostensibly complex nature, this report distills such sophisticated themes into an accessible, educational journey. By unraveling the impacts and future prospects of AI in healthcare, this report promises an insightful and adventurous read that broadens your understanding on an essential global issue. A worthwhile investment, it directs your gaze towards the horizon of upcoming medical innovations and equips you with the knowledge to confidently navigate the future of healthcare.

Chapter 2. AI: Redefining Healthcare

The advent of AI technology has represented a significant shift across an array of sectors, and healthcare is no exception. The confluence of AI in healthcare now promises not only to revolutionize the way health conditions are diagnosed and treated but also to usher in an era of proactive prevention.

2.1. An Introduction to AI in Healthcare

Artificial Intelligence, a term once associated primarily with robotics and software development, is today seen at the cutting edge of advancements in healthcare. As an interdisciplinary field, AI utilizes techniques and theories from many areas such as mathematics, computer science, and psychology to imitate, augment, and even amplify human intelligence.

In healthcare, AI applications emerge in various forms, ranging from robot-assisted surgeries to virtual nursing assistants, administrative workflow assistance, and beyond. Join us now as we explore how AI finds its expression in healthcare, tackling challenges, and providing solutions the traditional systems might find arduous.

2.2. AI for Diagnostics

One of the most impactful roles AI plays in healthcare is in diagnosis. Machine Learning, a subset of AI, has the capability to learn patterns from a vast amount of data. Whether it be X-rays, MRI scans, or health history records, these machine learning algorithms are trained to analyze and evaluate such data, often resulting in earlier and more accurate detection of diseases.

For instance, AI algorithms have shown notable success in diagnosing skin cancer, sometimes matching or even outperforming dermatologists. This doesn't mean that doctors are being replaced, but rather, both parties can work hand in hand to provide better patient care. AI tools can minimize human error, streamline the process, and focus on most relevant data, thereby freeing doctors' time for challenging and complex cases.

2.3. AI in Treatment Protocols and Personalized Medicine

In addition to diagnostics, AI holds promise in designing more effective, individualized treatment protocols. Traditionally, the 'one size fits all' approach has dominated medical treatment. However, given the trending precision medicine approach, healthcare is segueing towards more personalized treatments.

AI's role in personalized or precision medicine orbits around the principle of 'right patient, right treatment, right time.' It involves the use of predictive analytics to study various patterns and probabilities in significant data clusters, using patient history, genomic data, lifestyle, environmental factors and more.

2.4. AI and Proactive Prevention

Beyond the realm of diagnostics and treatment, AI wields substantial merit for preventive measures as well. AI-powered wearables like fitness trackers and smartwatches are already in the mainstream, providing users with extensive health-based data including heart rate, sleep patterns, physical activity levels, and more.

With the ability to monitor health trends and issue alerts related to potential health problems, these AI-powered devices edge us closer to proactive healthcare. Moreover, wider spread use of AI-powered predictive analytics in population health management can help identify at-risk groups, enabling the healthcare system to prioritize prevention over cure.

2.5. Ethical Implications of AI

While AI's potential in healthcare seems vast, it is prudent to touch upon the ethical implications it brings along. As with any emerging technology, the use of AI in healthcare presents some serious ethical challenges around privacy, bias, and transparency among others. A balance needs to be struck between technological innovation, real-world application, and ethical considerations to ensure that AI is used in a responsible and beneficial manner in healthcare.

2.6. The Future of AI in Healthcare

As we step into the future, AI firmly holds increasing potential to change the healthcare landscape. While we are currently witnessing its early applications, the hoped-for future will see AI infused in every step of the healthcare journey, enhancing and transforming care delivery.

Whether it's augmenting already existing physician skill sets, or pushing the boundaries of diagnostics and therapies, AI seems set to redefine healthcare. The healthcare providers of tomorrow would not only use AI to treat patients better, but also utilize it as a tool to understand, monitor and manage population health.

In conclusion, as AI continues its steadfast infiltration into healthcare, understanding its functions, potentials, and implications will be crucial for healthcare professionals and laypersons alike. Robust examinations, instructions, and partnerships between healthcare professionals, technology developers, and policy-makers will ensure that the AI revolution in healthcare is harnessed for the

greater good of everyone involved. The journey has just begun, and
the future, it seems, is here.

Chapter 3. Diving into AI: A Fundamental Overview

If we are to navigate uncharted territories, we must first understand the vessel that is to take us there. In this case, this vehicle is Artificial Intelligence (AI), a sophisticated tool rapidly shaping our future. This chapter plunges into the basics of AI, its functionalities, types, and the pathways it opens, particularly in healthcare.

3.1. The Anatomy of AI

In simple terms, AI can be described as the capability of a machine to imitate human intelligence. This imitation can range from learning and solving problems to recognizing speech and making decisions. Essentially, AI represents machines behaving 'intelligently,' which can be broken down into two principal types: Narrow AI and Artificial General Intelligence (AGI).

Narrow AI refers to systems designed to execute specific tasks such as voice recognition or recommendation systems. In contrast, an AGI- a term coined by AI researcher Ben Goertzel, is a machine with the ability to understand and learn any intellectual task that a human being can carry out, implying a competency level that matches or even supersedes human performance.

3.2. AI Integrations into Healthcare

The burgeoning integration of AI into healthcare owes its acceleration to four key changes. First, the exponential increase in healthcare data has paved the way for AI applications to make sense of this substantial volume of information. Second, advancements in computing power make it practical to process such massive data. Third, improvements in machine learning techniques have enabled the development of applications that learn from and use data effectively. Finally, increased digitization of health records has created a ready supply of data for AI and machine learning algorithms.

3.3. AI in Disease Diagnosis

One critical area where AI is making a significant difference is disease diagnosis. Traditional methods of diagnosing diseases can be subject to human errors, affected by issues such as fatigue, workload, or even bias. Machine learning algorithms, on the other hand, can pore over patient data mined from electronic health records, scanning images, extracting meaningful patterns, and predicting probable diagnoses with astonishing accuracy. Examples of such AI applications include the detection of cancers from medical imaging and the prediction of risk factors for diseases like cardiovascular conditions, diabetes, and chronic kidney diseases.

3.4. AI in Treatment Protocols

Following diagnosis, the treatment selection is the next crucial step. Here, AI offers an immense contribution by creating personalized treatment plans based on patient-specific information. Using deep learning algorithms and complex predictive models, AI can recommend personalized treatment protocols, considering potential drug interactions and the patient's unique health context. Furthermore, AI's ability to analyze large datasets can enable the identification of patterns and correlations that can lead to novel treatment methodologies.

3.5. AI in Proactive Prevention

The power of AI is not only limited to treating existing conditions. Its real potential lies in the proactive prevention of diseases. Wearable sensors and devices can monitor a patient's health status in real-time and reliably predict any potential health risks, facilitating early intervention. Machine learning models can identify patterns and correlations from lifestyle data, enabling proactive prevention strategies.

AI has, indeed, come a long way from simply being a 'buzzword.' It represents a transformative force across various industries, most prominently in healthcare. As we understand more about its potential, we move further towards a future where AI-enabled healthcare could add invaluable years to human life, improve quality of life, and significantly reduce healthcare costs. Moreover, initiatives to demystify and democratize AI technologies could result in a more inclusive healthcare system. Despite the challenges and ethical concerns, AI's journey in healthcare seems adventurous, trailblazing a promising path towards optimal global healthcare.

Chapter 4. Machine Learning and Big Data in Medicine

As healthcare evolves more intricately into the digital realm, Machine Learning (ML) and Big Data play a monumental role in transforming medical care. Their convergence in this field is morphing not only the way diagnoses are established and treatments administered but also the overall costs and quality of patient care.

4.1. Understanding Machine Learning

Machine Learning, a subset of AI, leverages computational algorithms that improve over time through exposure to data. Simply put, ML algorithms learn from experience. This revolutionary technology trains itself on vast datasets and acquires the capability to predict or make decisions without being explicitly programmed to carry out these tasks. It offers insights and important correlations from a multitude of data points that would be otherwise overwhelming or imperceptible to a human observer.

Machine learning models are broadly divided into supervised, unsupervised, and reinforcement learning. Supervised learning uses known data-input and output pairs to find patterns that map inputs to outputs. Unsupervised learning finds hidden patterns or intrinsic structures in input data where target outputs are not known. Reinforcement learning, on the other hand, learns how to act to achieve a goal by taking actions in an environment to maximize some reward.

While ML applications are myriad, their integration in the healthcare domain has been transformative, powering clinical decision-making, drug development, patient monitoring, and disease prediction.

4.2. Big Data: Unleashing the Power of Information Overflow

In parallel, the rise of Big Data—extremely large datasets that can be analyzed computationally—has had a seismic impact on health practices. Features that characterize big data, often referred to as the "five Vs"—Volume, Velocity, Variety, Veracity, and Value—offer a new means of aggregating and interpreting health-related facts.

With healthcare systems producing huge volumes of data (Volume), at high speed (Velocity), in various forms like text, images, genetic codes, etc. (Variety), and needing the exactness of this processed data to be reliable (Veracity), the ultimate goal lies in extracting meaningful and actionable insights (Value).

Using big data, medical professionals get a multi-dimensional view of a patient's medical history, current treatments, genomic data—and plausibly—their future health trajectory.

4.3. Merging Machine Learning and Big Data in Healthcare

When these two worlds meet, that's when the magic happens. The amalgamation of machine learning and big data in medical care opens possibilities for personalized medicine, predictive analytics, and improved patient outcomes.

ML algorithms feed on the diverse, extensive health data sets and go to work. They identify patterns, make connections, predict outcomes, and enable early intervention. They bring the promise of precision medicine to life by honing in on intricate biological, behavioral, and environmental factors that influence health.

4.4. Precision Medicine and Predictive Analytics

ML tools help determine the precise interaction of numerous individual health determinants. They unravel the complex interplay of genomics, lifestyle choices, environmental factors, and existing diseases in health outcomes.

This personalized approach aids in transforming treatment protocols. It paves the way for medicines and treatments tailored specifically to the individual's genetic makeup and lifestyle, leading to improved treatment outcomes. Such application in Genomics enables us to move from a 'one-size-fits-all' approach to a more individual-specific care model.

For example, ML algorithms have identified specific gene patterns linked with certain forms of cancer, assisting in early diagnosis and tailored treatment strategies – a significant leap towards personalized oncology.

Predictive analytics, on the other hand, gives a forward-looking perspective to healthcare. ML models, using the colossal volume of medical and lifestyle data, predict disease risk and support clinicians, patients, and policymakers before the onset of symptoms. It can also predict potential readmissions and assist in reducing healthcare costs.

4.5. Radiology and Imaging

In the realm of Radiology and Imaging, ML is igniting a paradigm shift. Imaging techniques like X-rays, CT scans, MRIs are an integral part of diagnostics. However, the process of interpreting these images is complex and time-consuming. ML algorithms have emerged as an effective solution by enhancing image analysis and interpretation.

Whether detecting a small tumor in a scan or comparing images to thousands of other patient images to find patterns, machine learning holds immense potential to streamline and enhance these tasks. Research suggests that ML models can read mammograms with similar accuracy to clinicians, improving efficiency and maximizing the chances of early detection.

4.6. Drug Discovery and Development

Another exciting frontier where ML and Big Data are making strides is drug discovery and development. Traditionally, this process is painstakingly long, expensive, and involves high attrition rates. ML algorithms, however, provide a faster, more efficient approach.

ML platforms can probe vast genetic, biomedical, and clinical databases to identify potential drug targets. They can also predict how different compounds might interact with these targets and forecast any possible adverse effects. Some algorithms can even design new molecules for potential drugs.

In battling the COVID-19 pandemic, ML models played a crucial role. They helped identify potential treatments repurposed from existing drugs and assisted in generating novel vaccines, thus significantly compressing the typically elongated timelines of drug discovery.

4.7. Future Prospects and Challenges

The benefits of using ML and Big Data in healthcare are considerable, and we're only at the cusp of what's possible. Predictive preventive care could reduce the burden of diseases significantly. Real-time monitoring and early interventions can cut down healthcare costs, and personalized treatment can improve patient outcomes.

However, integrating these technologies into healthcare isn't without its challenges. Issues regarding data privacy, algorithmic bias, lack of transparency, and explainability persist. Ensuring the equitable application of these tools is equally pressing.

Any discussion on AI in healthcare is incomplete without a reference to ethics laws and regulations. Given the sensitive nature of health data and the potentially life-altering implications of AI's predictions and decisions, adhering to medical ethics and data privacy laws is paramount.

Despite these challenges, the intersection of ML and Big Data in healthcare gives us reason for optimism. The blend of these two powerful technologies promises to reinvent the diagnostic and therapeutic landscape, propelling us further towards a future where health care is proactive, predictive, personalized, and precise.

As Medicine plunges deep into the digital era, ML and Big Data are poised to transform lives and redefine the boundaries of what is currently perceived as possible in healthcare. With continued innovation, what seems like science fiction today might just become our tomorrow's reality. No doubt, Machine Learning and Big Data hold an incredible key to the future of medicine. Their revolution in healthcare is just beginning. The best is yet to come.

Chapter 5. AI in Diagnostic Medicine: More Than a Second Opinion

Artificial intelligence (AI) has slowly been weaving its way into the intricacies of diagnostic medicine, providing invaluable insights that add to, and often surpass, the conventional 'second opinion'. Its multifaceted involvement ranges from machine learning to image analysis, predictive modeling, and so much more.

5.1. AI, Machine Learning, and Diagnostics

Machine learning, a subset of AI, is a technique that allows machines to evolve based on data inputs. In diagnostic medicine, machine learning specifically can offer significant enhancements. Imagine a machine capable of processing multitudes of health data points with precision, speed, and the capability of recognizing patterns faster than any human could do accurately. This is the reality unfolding within the healthcare sector today.

Understanding the fundamentals of machine learning is done by distinguishing between two of its critical components – supervised and unsupervised learning. Supervised learning utilizes known input and output data to predict future outputs. For instance, by analyzing thousands of patient chest x-rays alongside diagnoses, a machine can learn to correlate the image features with the presence or absence of a disease, thus making future diagnoses based on new inputs.

Unsupervised learning, on the other hand, explores input data without predefined outputs. The machine is left to find structure and relationships in the data on its own. Often, this leads to fascinating insights and novel medical discoveries.

5.2. Image Analysis and Its Potential

AI excels in analyzing medical imagery. It digests large volumes of medical images, then pairs them with case histories to derive patterns indicative of specific conditions. For example, algorithms have been developed to analyze CT scans of lungs, distinguishing benign nodules from malignant ones — often with superior accuracy to trained radiologists. Similarly, AI can minutely dissect pathological slides, identifying markers that could be missed by a human examiner.

This level of image analysis is culminated into AI tools such as Google's LYNA (Lymph Node Assistant). This AI system has demonstrated an ability to identify metastatic cancer with a 99% accuracy rate, outperforming human pathologists who, under pressure of time and workload, may miss minute, yet critical details.

5.3. Predictive Modelling in Disease Outbreaks

Another facet where AI proves invaluable is in predicting and managing disease outbreaks. By analyzing a plethora of data points including travel patterns, climate data, population density and health reports, AI has helped predict outbreaks of diseases such as Zika, Ebola and dengue. Moreover, given the recent global outbreak of COVID-19, AI predictive models went into overdrive, providing critical contributions in forecasting infection hotspots, hospital needs, and potential policy impacts.

5.4. Diagnosing Rare Diseases Using AI

Diagnostics is not restricted to common diseases alone. AI has been reliable in diagnosing rare diseases that often stump medical professionals due to their lower incidence rates. By scrutinizing unstructured data from sources such as health records, genetic information, and relevant literature, AI can piece together the diagnostic puzzle of rare diseases — an incredible step forward in precision medicine.

5.5. The Broadening Horizon of AI in Diagnostics

AI's role in diagnostic medicine isn't static. It is diversifying and deepening. Apart from the areas discussed, AI is making strides in early-stage disease detection, genomics, neurology, and optimization of treatment plans.

However, several critical issues must be addressed to ensure the sustainable integration of AI in diagnostics. These worries include data privacy and security, the requirement of vast annotated datasets, the explainability of AI decisions or 'black box' problem, and ethical considerations tied to machine-made decisions.

Despite these challenges, one cannot discount the enormous potential AI holds for enhancing diagnostic precision, efficiency, and patient outcomes. Hence, as we tread this exhilarating path of AI integration in diagnostic medicine, a cautious yet open-minded approach is indispensable.

Chapter 6. The AI Surgeon: Revolutionizing Surgical Precision

The future has manifested in the contemporary operating room, no longer a realm of solely human prowess but also mechanical precision, flexibility and ingenuity. We observe the emergent role of Artificial Intelligence (AI) in the surgery suite that tremendously heightens the precision, safety, and efficacy of surgical operations.

6.1. AI in the Operation Theatre: An Introduction

AI-driven surgical technologies comprise computer-assisted surgical systems, robotic assistants, and intricate algorithms that aid surgeons in preoperative planning, intra-operative decision making, and postoperative evaluation. As AI technology evolves, it will progressively revolutionize surgery, rendering highly intricate procedures safer and more accessible.

Imagine the space of a surgical operation. Ordinary humans cannot perform surgery flawlessly every single time due to natural limitations. However, imagine a robot unaffected by fatigue, tremors or even emotions, operating tirelessly for extended periods with remarkable steadiness. High precision, consistency, and capability for minimally invasive procedures are hallmarks of such AI-assisted interventions.

6.2. Robots Guided by AI: Unparalleled Precision

The first integral aspect in organically incorporating AI into surgery is robotic surgery assistants. Consider the Da Vinci surgical system, an AI-equipped robot that has performed millions of surgeries worldwide since its release. These systems offer surgeons enhanced visualization, superior precision, improved access to hard-to-reach organs, and the potential to perform complex surgeries less invasively.

Although not autonomous, these robots are anthropomorphic, mimicking human hands but with a greater range of motion. The surgeon essentially 'pilots' the robot, manipulating its arms from a high-definition 3D console, amplifying the surgeon's skills and reducing even the possibility of human error. Therefore, AI technology enables robotic surgeons to perform less invasive, more precise surgeries.

6.3. Preoperative Planning: Paving Path for Success

AI algorithms provide surgeons with predictive analytics, offering a detailed prognosis even before surgery. Accurate preoperative planning facilitated by AI includes interpreting radiographs, CT scans, or MRI data. This reduces the unpredictability of surgery, minimizing potential risks.

Examples include algorithms that predict the likelihood of successfully achieving negative margins in breast conserving surgery, or AI models predicting the risk of complications in spinal surgery. Predictive modelling in trauma surgery helps anticipate patient needs and outcomes given the precise medical history, injuries sustained, and recommended treatment procedures.

6.4. Perioperative Decision Making: Decoding Intraoperative Complexities

AI algorithms can decipher real-time changes in patient's condition during surgery, aiding surgeons with real-time decision making. Image-guided surgery powered by AI can highlight critical structures like blood vessels or specific organ parts that cannot be easily visualized. This helps surgeons make precise incisions and avoid harming vitals.

AI can assess variables like blood loss, body temperature, and patients' vitals during surgery, providing real-time feedback about whether the procedure is proceeding as planned or if alterations are necessary. This perioperative phase decision making is significant as it can potentially reduce the incidence of surgical morbidity and mortality.

6.5. Postoperative Evaluation and Follow-up: Optimizing Recovery

Once the surgery concludes, AI boosts postoperative care, enhancing recovery and minimizing complications. It can predict patient outcomes, alerting medical teams to possible complications like infections, readmissions, or adverse reactions. This way, AI-based systems can track patient recovery and aid in adjusting postoperative care plans if required.

AI algorithms also power telemedicine platforms, facilitating follow-up consultations, thereby reducing unnecessary hospital visits, potentially improving access to surgical care, and optimizing healthcare resources.

In essence, the 'AI Surgeon' possesses multi-faceted capabilities, streamlining the entire surgical journey from preoperative planning, intra-operative decision making to postoperative care, promising a transformative future. The narrative is evolving, the once supposed 'buzzword' is on route to becoming a healthcare mainstay, altering our perception of surgical precision, safety, and accessibility. As we continue our foray into the AI+Healthcare landscape, let's watch this space, for the incisions are crisp and the sutures, seamless.

Chapter 7. AI in Pharmacology: Personalizing Medication

Before delving into the detail, it's crucial to understand that pharmacology is a branch of medicine that encompasses the study of drugs or pharmaceuticals where the primary focus is the therapeutic application and potential toxicity of these substances. With the immense aid of AI, we witness a new era where the field is ushering towards personalized medication, shaping itself to serve the individualistic needs of patients. Let's traverse through this intriguing junction where AI and pharmacology meet.

7.1. The Concept: Personalized Medication

Personalized medication, an emerging approach, ultimately aims to tailor drug therapy by leveraging individual genetic makeup. Genetically defined subgroups may exhibit varying responses when exposed to identical medical treatments. This variance stems from the fact that our genes hold the key to how our bodies break down and absorb medication. By decoding this individual genetic information, personalized medication hopes to optimize drug therapy outcomes, bypassing the one-drug-fits-all treatment.

7.2. AI in Personalized Medication: The Bridge

With the expansive possibilities that AI brings, it serves as a potent bridge to the goal of personalized medication. It navigates through the dense genetic information that humans generate, identifying patterns that are almost invisible to the human eye.

AI models are trained on vast datasets, integrating multiple layers of biological information, including genomic, transcriptomic, and epigenetic data. With diverse datasets, AI can deduce intricate patterns that depict a comprehensive image of an individual's health profile.

Machine learning algorithms, a subset of AI, is used to analyze genetic factors that influence drug response. These algorithms can anticipate the optimal drug choice for a patient by comparing their genetic profile to an established database.

Deep learning, another AI subset, takes this a step further. By training on enormous datasets, this technology can learn to recognize layers of data patterns to predict how a person might respond to a drug.

7.3. Case Study: AI in Oncology Pharmacogenomics

AI has been most transformative in oncology pharmacogenomics. Cancer is a disease of the genome, and each tumor type has a unique genetic signature that may vary even within the same patient. AI offers a precise way to decode these signatures.

A prime example is IBM's AI, Watson, which has been deployed in oncology to guide therapeutic decisions. Watson can scrutinize vast amounts of medical literature and databases to match individual patient's molecular signatures with potential therapeutic agents, significantly reducing the time physicians spend on research.

7.4. The Promise and Perils of AI in Personalized Medication

AI promises several advantages in personalized medication. The most potent of all is the precise directive it provides for drug design and selection, saving valuable time, resources, and most importantly, lives. It paves the way for improved clinical outcomes with the reduced likelihood of side effects.

However, few challenges stand glaringly in the face of this pursuit. Privacy and ethical issues lurk around the handling and analysis of personal genomic data. Furthermore, the execution of personalized medicine requires significant computational power and adequate technical expertise. The digital divide may hinder equal access to such services.

AI-based personalized medication is still in its nascent stage, demanding robust clinical validation and regulatory benchmarks. A more comprehensive translational approach is necessary to harmonize the potential advantages with the above challenges.

7.5. Future Outlook

It's undoubtedly optimistic. Scientists foresee AI playing a pivotal role in moving personalized medication from the fringes of science into mainstream medicine. AI has the potential to unravel hidden patient patterns and trajectories buried within big healthcare data.

As data privacy legislation and AI models evolve, they hold the means to strengthen the infrastructure for personalized medication, enabling it to be the norm in the future.

AI in pharmacology nudges us closer to an era where treatment is no longer a generalized approach, but a protocol that recognizes and respects the individual's unique genetic makeup. In this journey towards personalizing medication, AI provides powerful tools that catalyze the revolution in healthcare.

Chapter 8. Ethical Considerations of AI in Healthcare

To start with, it's crucial to remember that every promising technological leap forward brings with it a spectrum of ethical considerations, and AI in healthcare is no exception to this rule. These considerations spawn from the potential of AI to either enrich or deleteriously impact the human experience in an unequal manner, thereby disrupting the balance of societal and individual ethics.

8.1. Ethical Concerns - An Overview

Foremost among the ethical concerns engendered by AI applications in healthcare are those surrounding the questions of fairness, justice, and equity. With AI systems being increasingly responsible for making health-related decisions, what guarantees do we have that these are bias-free? The problematic issue extends to the data which these applications utilize as raw material: is this data representative of the vast mosaic of human demographics, or do they inadvertently embed existing biases?

Moreover, the tension between machine autonomy and human oversight is palpable in the healthcare context. While AI is stepping in for routine tasks and complex diagnostics alike, there are concerns surrounding the degree of human involvement necessary to ensure ethics are upheld. Balancing this condition calls for developing prudent mechanisms of accountability and transparency within AI systems.

8.2. Bias in Medical AI Systems

AI systems are only as good as the data they're trained on. Given immense datasets available for training purposes, the potential for hidden or accidental bias is looming. Whether the skew is towards a particular gender, race, socio-economic group, or age group, such biases can seriously compromise the fairness and justice of AI applications in healthcare.

For instance, an AI system trained predominantly on data from a specific ethnic group may not perform as effectively on others. This not only leads to unequal quality in healthcare services but also exacerbates existing disparities, spinning a cycle of bias reproduction.

The scale of this issue pronounces the importance of ensuring data diversity. To make AI systems more equitable, it is imperative that the datasets used for training represent the broad demographic spectrum.

8.3. Autonomy Vs. Oversight: Balancing the Scales

AI technologies present considerable potential for automation in healthcare. While this undeniably offers many advantages, ethical questions arise about the need to maintain human oversight and intervention where necessary.

This questions are particularly pertinent in contexts like AI-driven medical diagnosis or treatment recommendations. Algorithmic output cannot always account for the subtleties of human biology, or the nuances of patients' values and preferences. Human oversight can provide the much needed 'sense-check' to balance autonomy with the safeguards integral to healthcare delivery.

On the other hand, over-dependence on human oversight risks stunting the potential benefits of AI. The balance, thus, is delicate and the equilibrium must be thoughtfully configured.

8.4. Accountability and Transparency in AI

The prospect of AI systems making errors in healthcare is daunting. Be it a faulty diagnosis or an incorrect treatment recommendation, the consequences could be severe. Here, the issue of accountability arises. How do we hold someone, or rather something, accountable for potentially life-changing decisions?

Furthermore, the inherent opaqueness of some AI systems, often termed 'black box' due to their inaccessible internal workings, brings forth the question of transparency. Most regulations governing healthcare uphold the principle of patient autonomy, mandating the providers to explain to the patient the basis of their diagnosis or treatment. Can AI systems meet this requirement?

Both transparency and accountability can instil trust in AI technologies among patients and health providers. This calls for the developers to design systems to be explainable, and for regulatory bodies to formulate prudent laws to maintain accountability.

8.5. Consent and Privacy

With digital data being the lifeblood of AI systems, concerns related to patient privacy and consent come to fore. These technologies often require extensive personal health data, raising questions around data security and patient confidentiality.

If AI applications use data collected from patients in routine settings, are patients adequately informed about its usage? How does the introduction of AI systems affect informed consent procedures?

Rigorous protection and regulation of patient data is a necessary prerequisite for realising the potential of AI in healthcare, achieving a balance between technological advancement and ethical commitment.

8.6. The Promise of Ethical AI

Potentially, developing AI systems for healthcare carries the inherent promise of generating significant improvements in patient outcomes — an ethically desirable objective that is worth striving for. However, it is crucial that the onward march of technology is accompanied by an equally robust evolution of ethical standards and considerations.

In conclusion, the advance of AI in healthcare raises several pressing ethical issues, many still unanswered due to the novelty of this domain. Yet, addressing these questions is vital, because a future where AI in healthcare is ubiquitous seems inevitable. As these systems become integral to our vanguard against disease and human frailty, ensuring their development and deployment are guided by a comprehensive ethical framework becomes of paramount importance. After all, the ultimate objective is a healthcare system that serves all sections of society equitably, grounded in the principles of fairness, justice, and respect for individual autonomy.

Chapter 9. AI and The Future of Mental Health

The mental health sector has long been stigmatized and under-resourced. For decades, we have seen the need for effective and accessible mental health treatment growing, often unsatisfied by existing resources. However, the advent of artificial intelligence (AI) is poised to potentially address this critical gap in global healthcare. Harnessing the power of AI-related technology has the potential to facilitate quicker, more accurate diagnostics and personalized therapeutic approaches, leading to a future where dealing with mental health issues could become less of a challenge.

9.1. Unmasking Mental Health with AI

To provide context, mental health disorders are one of the leading causes of disability worldwide, accounting for approximately one-third of years lost due to disability among adults. Anxiety and depressive disorders are among the most common, affecting hundreds of millions of individuals globally. Traditional diagnosis and treatment approaches often fail to provide comprehensive care to these individuals, leading to low recovery rates and high treatment costs, both economically and personally.

AI technologies, such as machine learning (ML) and natural language processing (NLP), hold the promise of transforming this landscape. These technologies can parse verbose volumes of data, identifying patterns and correlations that a human eye may miss, and potentially predict mental health issues even before they fully manifest.

Machine learning algorithms, fed with sufficient quality data, can match and even surpass human-level performance in diagnostic accuracy. For instance, in a 2019 study, ML algorithms developed by scientists were able to predict which patients would develop psychosis with 93% accuracy, vastly outperforming traditional diagnostic processes.

Natural language processing, another key AI technology, analyzes the nuances of human language, allowing for potential breakthroughs in understanding and diagnosing mental health issues. For instance, preliminary studies have found that individuals suffering from cognitive impairments, such as dementia, may show changes in their writing style before other symptoms become apparent. NLP can analyze these subtle linguistic shifts, providing early insights into deteriorating mental health conditions.

9.2. AI-Powered Therapy and Support

AI also holds significant potential in treatment interventions. Chatbots and digital therapeutic solutions that utilize AI show promising results in providing cost-effective, accessible, and stigma-free mental health support. For example, Woebot, a cognitive behavioral therapy (CBT) chatbot, has proven to be effective in reducing symptoms of anxiety and depression in young adults.

Digital therapeutics like these have become increasingly robust, offering layers of support for users. They can provide in-the-moment coping strategies, therapeutic exercises, and even full-fledged courses on cognitive-behavioral therapy themes. Perhaps most importantly, digital care reduces the financial toll of mental health care and circumvents the pervasive issue of treatment stigma, making it more accessible to the general population.

9.3. Shrinking the Mental Health Treatment Gap

Globally, it's estimated that about 60% of individuals with a mental disorder do not receive the treatment they need, largely due to issues of access. AI not only improves the quality of care but also remarkably expands the reach of mental health services.

Telepsychiatry or online therapy, bolstered by AI innovations, are becoming effective mediums for mental health service delivery to remote or underserved communities. Online platforms provide the merits of convenience, accessibility, and anonymity, which can be significant to individuals seeking help, especially in regions stigmatized against mental health conditions.

9.4. The Ethics of AI in Mental Health

The promises of AI in mental health are significant, but they also warrant careful ethical considerations. Data privacy and security is a primary concern. Sensitive mental health data are an attractive target for cyberattacks. Therefore, strong data encryption and privacy protocols are paramount to any AI solution in this field.

Prioritizing ethics in AI requires incorporating fundamental principles such as transparency, inclusivity, fairness, and accountability in the design and deployment of AI systems. Furthermore, there's the need for regulation and legal frameworks that account for AI's unique dynamics while protecting patients' rights and interests.

9.5. AI: Shaping the Future of Mental Health

While still in its formative stages, the integration of AI into mental health care holds strong promise for the future. Its potential to revolutionize diagnosis, treatment, and healthcare accessibility positions AI as an influential factor in shaping the future of mental health. Nevertheless, the path forward necessitates a careful balance between technological advancements and ethical considerations.

On the whole, as we stand on the brink of an AI-powered paradigm shift in mental health care, the importance of adeptly navigating the nuances of this innovative frontier becomes increasingly paramount. By continuing to explore, learn, and improve, we can harness the power of AI to better address global mental health challenges, ultimately providing better outcomes for those in need.

Chapter 10. Breaking Barriers: AI in Global Healthcare

Despite the initial apprehensions about AI stepping into the sanctum of healthcare, this technology has successfully broken down barriers, creating a comprehensive, collaborative and global platform. AI's journey, while revolutionary, has only just begun. Although we are already witness to substantial transformations in healthcare, this is merely the precursor for what's yet to come.

10.1. Impact of AI on Global Healthcare

The global health sector is on the cusp of a revolution, with artificial intelligence promising to bring radical changes. Hospitals, clinics, and medical practitioners around the world are rapidly recognizing the potential of AI to improve operational efficiency, diagnostic accuracy, therapy customization, and patient care.

AI applications range from simple systems that aid the administrative tasks of medical facilities, to complex algorithms that can read CT scans, MRIs, and other medical imagery better than human medical professionals. AI is perceived not as a replacement for human intervention, but as a reliable ally that can complement and significantly enhance human expertise.

10.2. AI Technologies Transforming Healthcare

Today, AI has influenced a myriad of areas within healthcare, beginning from administrative tasks to complex surgical procedures. Some of the technologies drastically altering the healthcare landscape include Machine Learning, Natural Language Processing, Robotics, and Computer Vision.

Machine learning algorithms have been instrumental in predicting patient readmissions, potential complications, and risk factors. These implications not only save millions of dollars for health systems but also significantly contribute to improving patient outcomes.

Natural language processing empowers health systems to draw meaningful information from diverse patient data. This technology is helping providers improve patient care, facilitate accurate diagnosis, and even make predictions about a patient's future health risks.

Robotic surgery has become a reality with the progress of AI technologies. Surgeons are now using robotic systems to perform precise, controlled operations, minimizing human error and vastly improving the success rate of complex surgeries.

Computer vision in healthcare is revolutionizing diagnostics by training machine learning models on thousands of medical images. This allows AI to successfully diagnose a range of conditions, sometimes with greater accuracy than human professionals.

10.3. Overcoming Challenges with AI in Healthcare

Although AI has demonstrated potential to dramatically change healthcare, it must overcome numerous challenges before its full potential can be realized. These challenges include data privacy concerns, ethical quandaries, a lack of interpretability of AI algorithms and resistance from healthcare professionals who question the reliability of AI technology.

However, AI can provide a solution to some of these challenges. Data privacy concerns can be mitigated by using AI algorithms that anonymize patient data. Ethical issues can be addressed with the development of AI regulations. Explainability of AI can be improved by advances in AI transparency initiatives. Lastly, the distrust among healthcare professionals can be resolved by building robust AI systems, continuous training and testing, and transparent communication around the capabilities and limitations of AI.

10.4. Future Prospects: AI's Growing Influence

Looking ahead, the influence of AI in healthcare is projected to increase exponentially. AI could soon power virtual health assistants that can monitor patient health in real time, predict health risks, and provide advice on preventive care. Gene-based personal therapy could also be delivered with the help of AI.

Furthermore, AI is anticipated to play a critical role in breaking down health disparity barriers. It could make healthcare more accessible and affordable for underprivileged populations by providing diagnostic support, identifying treatment options, and assessing disease risks.

AI is also expected to form the backbone of pandemic preparedness and response, predicting and monitoring outbreaks, assessing population health risks, and aiding in public health decision-making.

In conclusion, the future of global healthcare lies in AI's capable hands. As we navigate the challenges and possibilities that AI presents, its integration into healthcare must be deliberative and strategic. With each barrier it breaks, AI brings us closer to a future where healthcare is more personalized, effective, and accessible universally.

Chapter 11. Envisioning the Future: Prospects and Challenges of AI in Health

In an era where technology reigns supreme, the crossroads of AI and healthcare holds profound implications for our future. These ramifications span across various dimensions, from the accurate detection of diseases to effectual treatment protocols to proactive health management strategies. However, along with the myriad of opportunities AI presents, the path forward isn't devoid of challenges. It is indispensable for us to recognize these hurdles for effective mitigation and capitalization on these cutting-edge innovations.

11.1. The Advent of AI in Healthcare: An Overview

Artificial intelligence's inception into healthcare has embarked on an era of precision medicine, where diagnosis and treatments are not a one-size-fits-all approach, but are tailored to each individual. Machine learning - an AI subset, sifts through vast quantities of health data, learning patterns that often escape human eyes. Complex algorithms are developed based on these patterns that can predict the possibility of diseases, enhancing early detection. For instance, a Harvard Medical School study demonstrated how AI could anticipate breast cancer nearly five years before it appeared. The imminence of such protocols can potentially revolutionize early detection, effectively increasing the chances for successful treatments.

AI in healthcare also extends into devising optimized treatment plans. Google's DeepMind developed a model that accurately predicted the 3D shapes of proteins. Unraveling these shapes can help scientists understand diseases better and create effective molecular strategies to combat them. Furthermore, AI can potentially streamline healthcare operations, optimizing resource allocation, and thus amplifying efficiency.

11.2. The Future Outlook of AI in Healthcare

The future of AI in healthcare is expansive, with potential applications transcending the current uses. AI technology could facilitate adaptive and intelligent health surveillance systems, which not only respond to outbreaks but predict and prevent them. Imagine a world where pandemics could be detected and responded to before they spread - a feat which is potentially feasible with AI.

In terms of individual health management, we could witness the growth of personalized healthcare AI interfaces. These algorithm-driven platforms could monitor real-time health data, make dietary suggestions, advise on lifestyle changes, or even warn of imminent health issues.

Further, the neural networks of AI could boost mental health treatments by identifying patterns in speech, texts, or social media activities that might indicate possible disorders. Teletherapy, aided by AI, can provide affordable and accessible help for individuals who can't visit a professional in person, bridging the gap between treatment demand and supply.

11.3. The Challenges and Limitations of AI

However, the application and integration of AI in healthcare isn't absent hurdles. The path is replete with challenges that we need to address for AI to make a substantive, sustainable difference.

One major concern is patient data privacy. With AI systems requiring massive datasets to improve accuracy, there are understandable worries about data mishandling or misuse. Implementing robust data protection mechanisms is vital to hopefully alleviate these concerns.

Another challenge is algorithm biases. An AI's efficiency entirely depends on the data it learns from. Biased data can lead to biased outcomes, which might impact the quality of care directly. Strategies to reduce biases in training data can help ensure AI systems are accurate, reliable, and equitable.

AI also encumbers the 'Explainability' problem - its decision-making process is intricate, which can be a black box to humans, impacting users' trust. Efforts to enhance algorithm transparency can bridge this trust gap, enabling healthcare professionals to understand and evaluate AI system outputs themselves.

Lastly, there's an acute need for regulation and evaluation protocols. Although AI holds significant promise in health sectors, protocols to regulate and evaluate AI systems are paramount to ensuring public safety and fostering innovation.

11.4. Mitigating Challenges for AI Success in Healthcare

To reap the benefits AI offers, we must address these challenges. Regulations that protect patient data while still enabling innovation are necessary. Policies should focus on regulating how data is used, rather than limiting data collection.

To tackle algorithmic bias, diversity in data samples collected is crucial. Healthcare systems must pull from various demographics and locations to develop algorithms that provide quality care for all.

Transparency in AI decisions can be developed by adding interpretability into AI models. This allows healthcare professionals to understand AI decisions, boosting their confidence in the technology.

A standardized evaluation protocol, ensuring AI systems' safety, efficacy, trustworthiness is vital. Consistent, rigorous, and independent assessments can help guarantee that only reliable and helpful AI systems are deployed in healthcare.

The opportunities and challenges AI presents in healthcare marks the dawn of an era that aspires to revolutionize our health trajectories. As we journey through this impending frontier, acknowledging these challenges, and proactively seeking solutions is the optimal path forward. This emerging synthesis of AI and healthcare heralds the promise of a healthier future, if conscientiously managed, navigated, and regulated. Now more than ever, the future of healthcare lies in our ability to form a symbiotic relationship between man and machine.